@RosenTeenTalk

Life Skills

SELF-CARE IRL

Kathleen A. Klatte

ROSEN PUBLISHING

Published in 2025 by The Rosen Publishing Group, Inc.
2544 Clinton Street, Buffalo, NY 14224

First Edition

Editor: Greg Roza
Designer: Rachel Rising

Photo Credits: Cover, pp. 1, 3, 5, 45 Miljan Zivkovic/Shutterstock.com; Cover Cosmic_Design/Shutterstock.com; Cover, pp. 1, 3–48 Vitya_M/Shutterstock.com; pp. 3, 17 ESB Professional/Shutterstock.com; pp. 3, 25, oneinchpunch/Shutterstock.com; pp. 3, 35 ponsulak/Shutterstock.com; pp. 3, 41 Rawpixel.com/Shutterstock.com; p. 6 svtdesign/Shutterstock.com; p. 7 Rawpixel.com/Shutterstock.com; p. 8 Djavan Rodriguez/Shutterstock.com; p, 9 noraismail/Shutterstock.com; p. 10 Platslee/Shutterstock.com; p. 11 Roman Samborskyi/Shutterstock.com; p. 13 KOTOIMAGES/Shutterstock.com; p. 14 Quang Ho/Shutterstock.com; p. 15 LightField Studios/Shutterstock.com; p. 16 Mariia Ahafonova/Shutterstock.com; p. 19 AlessandroBiascioli/Shutterstock.com; p. 20 LN_PHOTO/Shutterstock.com; p. 21 Parilov/Shutterstock.com; p. 22 trekandshoot/Shutterstock.com; p. 23 SeventyFour/Shutterstock.com; p. 24 Muqamba/Shutterstock.com; p. 26 kazuya goto/Shutterstock.com; p. 27 Ground Picture/Shutterstock.com; p. 29 BongkarnGraphic/Shutterstock.com; p. 30 Razym/Shutterstock.com; p. 31 PeopleImages.com - Yuri A/Shutterstock.com; p. 33 VH-studio/Shutterstock.com; p. 34 PremiumVector/Shutterstock.com; p. 35 Kicking Studio/Shutterstock.com; p. 36 ulegundo/Shutterstock.com; p. 37 SeventyFour/Shutterstock.com; p. 38 Dragon Images/Shutterstock.com; p. 39 Daniel Hoz/Shutterstock.com; p. 40 creativesunday/Shutterstock.com; p. 41 Chinnapong/Shutterstock.com; p. 42 mentalmind/Shutterstock.com; p. 43 Alena Divina/Shutterstock.com.

Some of the images in this book illustrate individuals who are models. The depictions do not imply actual situations or events.

Cataloging-in-Publication Data

Names: Klatte, Kathleen A.
Title: Self-care IRL / Kathleen A. Klatte.
Description: Buffalo, NY : Rosen Young Adult, 2025. | Series: @RosenTeenTalk: Life skills | Includes glossary and index.
Identifiers: ISBN 9781499477597 (pbk.) | ISBN 9781499477603 (library bound) | ISBN 9781499477610 (ebook)
Subjects: LCSH: Self-care, Health--Juvenile literature. | Well-being--Juvenile literature. | Caring--Juvenile literature.
Classification: LCC RA777.K525 2025 | DDC 613--dc23

Manufactured in the United States of America

CPSIA Compliance Information: Batch #CSRYA25. For Further Information contact Rosen Publishing at 1-800-237-9932.

CONTENTS

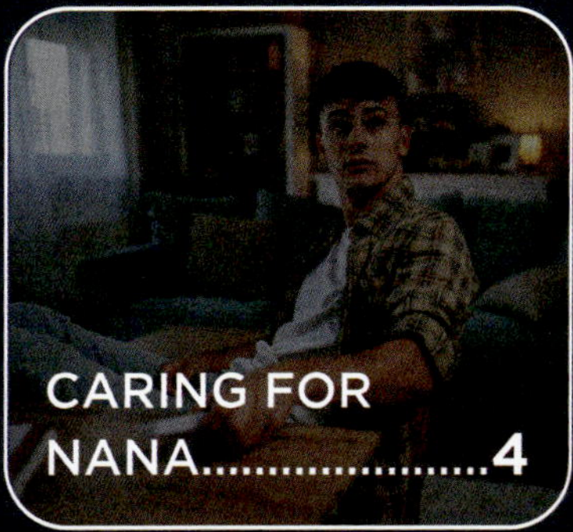

Chapter 1

Caring for Nana

It's been crazy at home lately. My Nana had a stroke. For a while we were scared she might die. She's better now, but she has to live in a nursing home. My folks have all sorts of extra stuff to do for Nana, so I've been trying to help.

I help my sister with her homework and do things around the house, but it's a lot with my own homework and stuff. And I worry about Nana too.

The social worker at the nursing home talked to us about something called self-care. They say it's important to take care of ourselves, not just other people. I'm not sure, though. It sounds selfish to take time for myself when my folks are so **stressed**.

It's easy to feel **overwhelmed** when there's a family **emergency**.

WHAT IS SELF-CARE?

Self-care is all the things we do to keep ourselves happy and healthy. It includes things that keep our bodies healthy, like eating, sleeping, and bathing. It includes things we do that make us happy, like spending time with our friends.

Self-care means different things to different people. What works for someone else might not be helpful for you. Self-care doesn't have to be fancy or expensive. It can be as simple as going for a walk in the fresh air.

Doing a puzzle or playing with a building toy gives you something to focus on besides what's worrying you.

BREAKING THE CYCLE

Sometimes our brains get stuck worrying about something. For some people, the best way to break the worry cycle is to give their brain something else to think about.

SELF-CARE ISN'T SELFISH

When we see someone in pain, it's natural to want to help. However, to be helpful to someone else, you first have to take care of yourself. When you use up too much of your energy on other people, it's not healthy. You can become tired and cranky. You might make mistakes. You can get sick or even injured. You definitely won't have as much patience for the person you're trying to help.

A car with an empty gas tank isn't going anywhere. A helper who's tired, hungry, or grouchy can't help anyone else.

GIVERS

Maybe you read the book *The Giving Tree*, by Shel Silverstein, when you were little. In the story, the tree gives the boy everything she has until all that's left is a stump. That can happen to people too. They can do things for other people until they're too tired to look after themselves.

You can't help other people unless you take care of yourself. You can't do well at school or a job if you're stressed or tired.

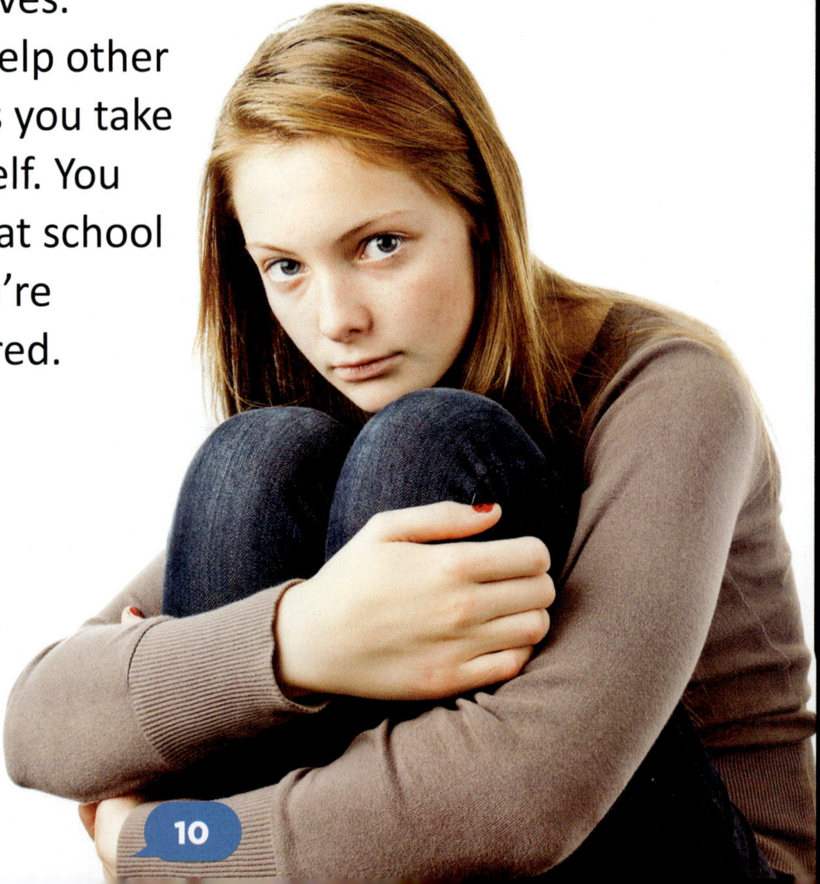

Whatever else is going on in your life right now, you need to take care of your body for your mind to work properly.

WHAT IF?

You have an exam in the morning. Your dad asked you to help clean out the garage after dinner. What do you think will help you do well on your exam?

A. staying up late cramming

B. helping your dad

C. getting a good night's sleep

Setting Boundaries

I've had the same bunch of friends since kindergarten. We've always done everything together. Lately, though, one of the girls—Marisol—has gotten to be kind of a jerk. She's really into hair and makeup. She says mean things about other girls. She thinks it's dumb to hang out at the comics shop or amusement park. She's really nasty to another friend who wears glasses and likes to read.

Makeup is fun for special occasions, but I don't want to spend hours in front of the mirror every day. And I still like comic books. I really don't want to be around someone who's a bully. I'm going to talk to Marisol. If she can't be nice to everyone in the group, I don't think I can be friends with her anymore.

You don't have to stay friends with someone who's being mean or doing things you really don't like. It's important to be open with your friends about your feelings.

SCHOOL STRESS

Self-care isn't just for adults. Kids need to take care of themselves too. School can be very stressful. You might be worried about exams, grades, and getting into college. Other kids might try to get you to do things like drink or try drugs. This is called peer pressure.

Active shooter drills and lockdown drills are terrifying. Sometimes you don't know until after that it's a drill. Hearing in the news that there was another school shooting is also very upsetting.

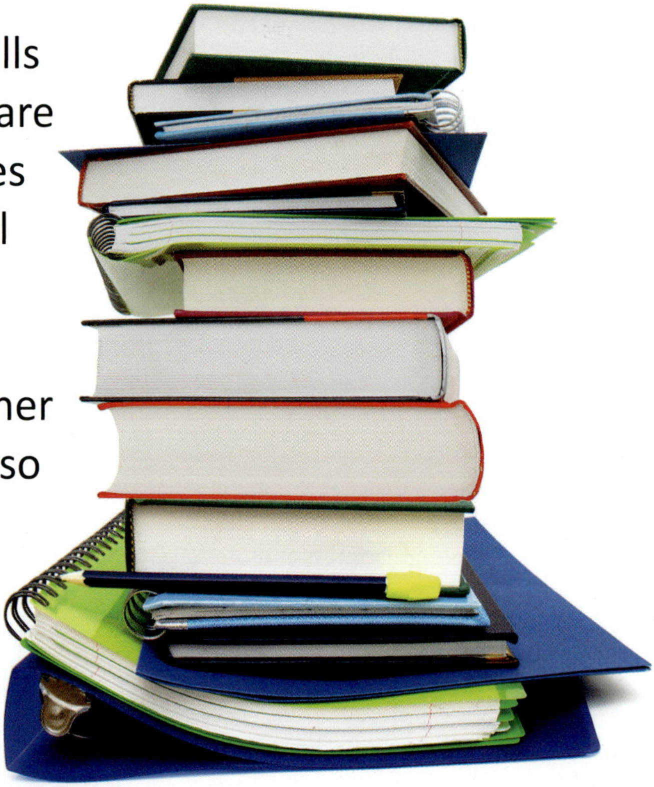

Keep in Mind...

Teens can feel more stressed out than adults because the part of the brain that deals with stress isn't fully developed yet.

There are stressful things in your life that your folks probably never had to worry about when they were your age, such as the recent COVID-19 **pandemic**. It's important for you to share your worries with your parents or another trusted adult.

CALMING ROOMS

Some schools are creating calming rooms. These are rooms with comfortable seating and low lighting. Students can go there to recover from **anxiety** or panic attacks.

Chapter 2

FRESH AIR AND SUNSHINE

One of the easiest and least expensive forms of self-care is getting fresh air and sunshine. Sunlight helps your body release a **hormone** called serotonin. This makes you feel happy. Sunlight also helps your body produce vitamin D, which helps keep you healthy.

Going outside for a walk, even just for fifteen minutes, can make you feel much better. Walking helps improve your blood circulation. Exercise and fresh air can also help you sleep better at night.

Did You Know?

Seasonal affective disorder (SAD) is a type of **depression**. It happens to some people during autumn and winter. Doctors believe it's connected to shorter days with less sunlight.

Even if you're studying for an exam or trying to finish a project, taking little breaks can help you work better and faster.

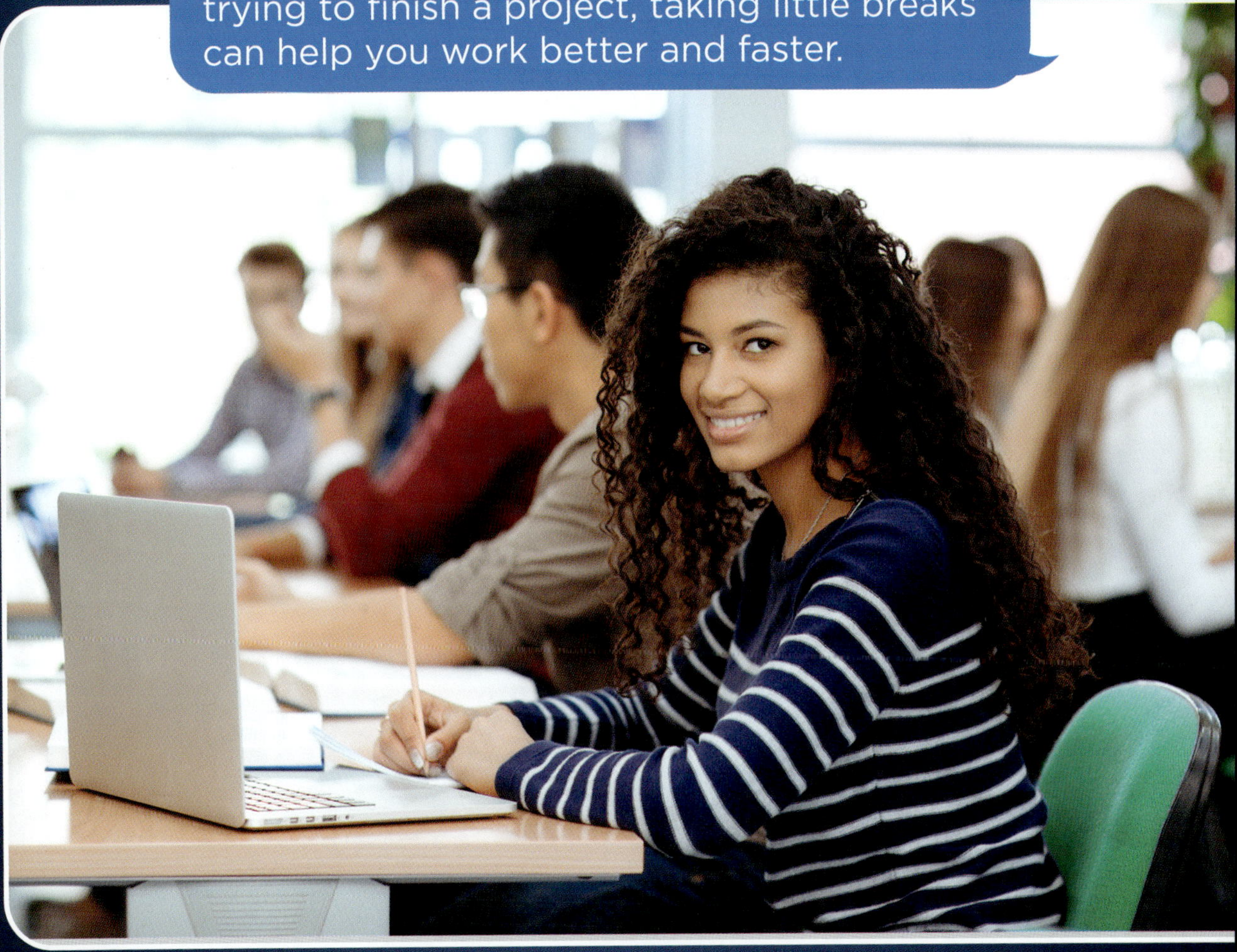

EATING RIGHT

Eating right is important for a healthy body. Teens' bodies grow very quickly and need a lot of fuel. When you skip meals or eat a lot of junk food, you don't have enough energy for your busy day.

A balanced diet includes:

- fruits
- vegetables
- grains
- meat
- fish
- dairy products
- other sources of protein

Eating a healthy diet helps you grow strong bones, teeth, and muscles. It also helps prevent problems like **heart disease** and **diabetes.**

Preparing and sharing a meal with people you love is a form of self-care. It makes both your mind and body happy.

GETTING ENOUGH REST

Getting enough sleep is one of the most important kinds of self-care. Most doctors think teens need nine or ten hours of sleep each night. Your body uses up a lot of energy because it's growing and changing so quickly.

Your body releases hormones when you sleep. This helps it to repair itself. It's also when your mind **organizes** memories. This is how you remember what you learned in school during the day.

The light from computer screens can disrupt your brain from winding down for sleep. **Experts** suggest putting away computer devices an hour before bedtime.

TAKE A BREAK

Getting enough rest is so important that some jobs require sleep breaks after a certain number of hours. Flight crews and **professional** drivers need to have breaks of eight to 12 hours between shifts so they can do their jobs safely.

TIDY UP

Cleaning up your space is a form of self-care that has many benefits.

- A clean space is healthier—it has less dust and allergens.
- An organized space helps you focus—if your things are put away, there's less competition for your attention.
- A tidy room helps you feel in control—even if there are big things happening in your life that you can't control, you can make your own space neat and comfortable.

It's impossible to concentrate or even find anything in a room like this. Plus it will make your folks cranky.

Did You Know?

Cleaning things (as well as doing other productive or enjoyable activities) releases endorphins. These are **chemicals** in your brain that make you feel good.

And of course, if you clean your room, your folks won't have to nag you about it. That makes everyone happier!

Chapter 3

DISCONNECT AND REFRESH

Social media can be lots of fun. It's great to post pictures of things you do or share funny memes with your friends. However, sometimes it's good to step away from the screen.

Constantly scrolling through your accounts can waste a lot of time. It also distracts you from more important things—such as homework, chores, or face-to-face time with friends.

If a major news story is breaking, the constant flow of updates and comments can be confusing—or sometimes just plain wrong. It's better to take a break and wait to get news from a **reputable** source.

Cyberbullying

Cyberbullying is when people use social media to be nasty to others. They may do things like tag you in a post about a party you weren't invited to. Cyberbullying is a good reason to disconnect from the internet.

It's important to make time to step away from the screen every day. Mindfulness is the practice of living in the moment. Get some fresh air and pay attention to the people around you.

TURN OFF THE NEWS

Today, news stories are reported on the internet right as they happen. Smartphones buzz with news alerts and push notifications pop up on computer screens.

It's good to be aware of what's happening in the world, but sometimes the constant stream of updates is just too much. It's important to turn off the news sometimes, especially if a major tragedy is being reported. It's not healthy to keep looking at upsetting pictures or hearing distressing news.

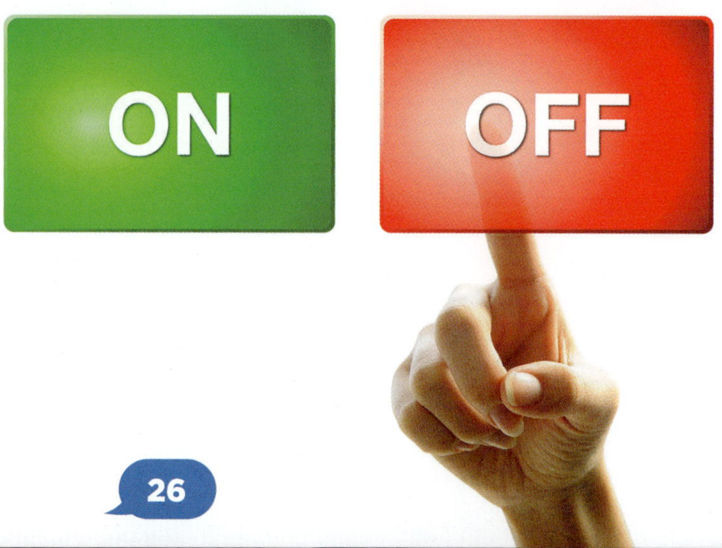

Stress Hormones

Constant **exposure** to upsetting news stories makes your body release stress hormones, such as cortisol and adrenaline.

Your folks need to take a break from the news sometimes too. If there's a really scary news story, sometimes it's best to watch a funny movie. Or turn off the TV entirely and play a board game together.

DOOMSCROLLING

Constantly looking through social media feeds and news alerts when there's an upsetting news story is called doomscrolling. "Doom" means a very bad situation that can't be avoided. But you CAN turn off the news and do something that makes you happy.

REFRESH YOUR SPIRIT

Life sometimes includes things that leave you feeling bruised inside. Little things like rudeness, small losses, and disappointments add up over time. Everyone needs a way to refresh their spirit. Some people take comfort from the prayers and rituals of formal religion. This might be the case if their whole family worships together.

Other people find calm in different ways. These might include:

- **meditation**
- journaling or drawing
- walking in a park or other natural place
- sitting in a quiet place like a library or museum

Everyone needs a little quiet time to unwind. Writing out your ideas in a journal can help clear your mind.

ENERGIZE YOUR BODY

Exercise is an important form of self-care. Exercising daily helps keep your body and mind healthy. It builds strong muscles and improves heart health. Exercise can also help prevent diseases like obesity (being overweight) and diabetes. It also produces endorphins, which we've already learned helps make you feel happy.

Playing a sport can be a great way to get exercise. You get the benefits of physical activity plus the fun of playing a game with your friends.

Just for Fun

At the high school level, sports can become very competitive. There might be practices every day after school and games every weekend. It's OK to step back if you just want to play for fun.

Playing sports for fun can be part of a happy, healthy lifestyle.

THE PRESIDENT'S COUNCIL ON SPORTS, FITNESS, AND NUTRITION

The President's Council on Sports, Fitness, and Nutrition is a government program designed to promote healthy living for all Americans. You can learn more at: health.gov/pcsfn

It's Not Fun Anymore

I used to love playing basketball. I'd go out with my friends after school and play in the park until dinner. Then I joined the school team. That was fun for a while, but lately it's become just another thing I have to do.

The coach wants me to try out for the varsity team, but I don't want to. Those girls are trying to get into college teams, then maybe even the pros. They're super intense about official practice every day and extra drills besides.

I like to do other things besides basketball. I want to go to vet school, so I need good grades. I also need to put in **volunteer** hours at an animal shelter or rescue because that'll look good to vet schools.

It doesn't matter how good other people think you are at a sport. You don't have to make it your top concern if it's not fun, or if there are other things you'd rather do.

Chapter 4

IT'S OK TO SAY NO

Teens go through a lot of changes. This includes their interests. Some of your friends might like books or movies with a lot of romance. Maybe this doesn't interest you. It might even make you uncomfortable. That's perfectly fine.

Or maybe "everyone" is watching that cool new show with zombies. Watching bloody shows might make you feel sick. Or maybe you just don't enjoy the show. You don't have to like the same things as everyone else. You don't owe anyone an explanation, either.

How to Just Say No

"No, thanks."

"I'm not interested in that."

"I'd rather watch (other movie) instead."

Blame your folks. "I'll be grounded if I do that."

Set up a "secret" way to ask for a ride home if you're in an uncomfortable situation. Some kids text their parents a specific word or character, like the poo emoji.

ME TIME

It's important to have quiet time to yourself. Everyone needs a little time alone to recharge. You might want to read a book just for fun or write in a journal. This can be difficult if you have brothers and sisters, or if you don't have your own room.

If you're not able to go in another room and close the door, you can try playing soft music or nature sounds on headphones to block out household noises.

It's important to have quiet time to study and do homework. It's also important to have time to yourself to read, listen to music, or work on a hobby.

FRIENDS AND FAMILY TIME

Self-care is all about finding balance in your life. Too much time alone is as bad as no privacy at all. It's important to spend time with your friends and family. Being together with people you care about can lessen your stress levels. When you're part of a social group you can talk about your problems instead of letting them build up inside your mind. This is good for your physical health too.

You can learn a lot from spending time with your older family members. Perhaps they lived in a different country or speak a second language. They're an important link to your culture.

Friends face many of the same challenges you’re going through. Sometimes they understand you better than your family.

Chapter 5

TIME MANAGEMENT

How do you do all the things you need to do to take care of yourself without going crazy? Time management is a form of self-care. For instance, don't try to complete a big project or study for an exam in one long session. Work for half an hour, then get up. Take five minutes to stretch your legs or get a glass of water. Your mind will be clearer and your work will be better.

A kitchen timer is a good way to break up your time into small, manageable chunks.

A day planner that you write in can help you plan out big projects ahead of time so you're not stressed trying to finish at the last minute.

A family chalk board can be a great way to keep track of everyone's activities—and make sure family time is included!

HEALTHY HABITS FOR LIFE

Learning good self-care habits now can help set you up for a happy and healthy future. According to a report by U.S. News and World Reports, eating right, exercising, and getting enough sleep as a teen helps your mind develop correctly. People who take good care of their bodies are less likely to develop depression. Taking good care of yourself when you're young can also lessen the chances of serious health issues when you're older.

Self-care is about finding balance in your life. You need time to be alone, time to be with other people, time to work or study, and time to relax.

Did You Know?

Notable magazines and newspapers, such as *Forbes* and *The Wall Street Journal*, have run articles on the importance of employees using all their vacation time. Studies have shown that workers who use all their time off are more productive, which means they get more done.

When you take time to eat, sleep, and relax, it makes it easier for you to concentrate on your schoolwork.

- [ ] skin care
- [ ] exercise
- [ ] read
- [ ] drink water
- [ ] eat healthy
- [ ] meditate
- [ ] listen to music
- [ ] sleep well
- [ ] talk to a friend

Caring for Myself

The social worker was right about this self-care stuff. If I take some time every day and go outside for a walk or throw a ball around, I feel better. I seem to get my homework done faster, too. And my little sister doesn't annoy me as much.

My folks are trying too. My mom bought some fancy bubble bath to help her relax. My dad turns his phone off while we have dinner, even if it's just takeout. They decided that they're not going to visit the nursing home every day. Saturday is going to be family day, just the four of us.

Now when we do go visit Nana, everyone is happier. We're not so tired and cranky, so we can sit and help her do puzzles or watch a movie. Even Nana seems happier!

Taking time to take care of yourself makes it easier for you to help others.

GLOSSARY

anxiety: Fear or nervousness about what might happen.

chemical: A substance (such as an element or compound) that is made by a chemical process.

depression: A state of feeling sad.

diabetes: A serious disease in which the body cannot properly control the amount of sugar in your blood because it does not have enough of a hormone called insulin.

emergency: An unexpected and usually dangerous situation that calls for immediate action.

expert: A person who has special skill or knowledge relating to a particular subject.

exposure: The state of being left open to view or otherwise take in some kind of stimulus.

heart disease: An abnormal condition of the heart or of the heart and circulation (such as coronary heart disease, arrhythmia, or heart-valve defect).

hormone: A natural substance that is produced in the body and that influences the way the body grows or develops.

meditation: The process or activity of spending time in quiet thought.

organize: To arrange or order things so that they can be found or used easily and quickly.

overwhelm: To affect (someone) very strongly.

pandemic: An occurrence in which a disease spreads very quickly and affects a large number of people over a wide area or throughout the world.

professional: Someone who does a job that requires special training, education, or skill; someone who is a member of a profession.

reputable: Respected and trusted by most people; having a good reputation.

stress: Something that causes strong feelings of worry or anxiety.

volunteer: A person who works without being paid; to work without pay; to offer service without being asked.

INDEX